SCAPE

Also by Joshua Harmon

Quinnehtukqut (2007)

SCAPE

Joshua Harmon

Black Ocean
Boston · New York · Chicago

Black Ocean
P.O. Box 52030
Boston, MA 02205

cover art by Dan McCarthy
www.danmccarthy.org

Library of Congress Cataloging-in-Publication Data

Harmon, Joshua, 1971–
  Scape / Joshua Harmon.
    p. cm.
  Poems.
  ISBN 978-0-9777709-8-4
  I. Title.

PS3608.A7485S33 2009
811'.6—dc22
2008055545

Printed in Canada

FIRST EDITION

for Sarah

ACKNOWLEDGMENTS

Some of these poems were first published, sometimes in different forms or under different titles, in *Colorado Review*, *Columbia*, *Denver Quarterly*, *Diagram*, *Gulf Coast*, *Handsome*, *Indiana Review*, *The Journal*, *jubilat*, *LIT*, *The New Criterion*, *Slope*, *Sonora Review*, *Verse*, and *Web Conjunctions*.

Many thanks to the following people for their help with these poems: Paige Ackerson-Kiely, Brian Henry, Jonathan Monroe, Allison Titus, Andrew Zawacki, and especially Sarah Goldstein.

The lines "nothing but in care of you" and "his arms in this sad knot" (p. 62) are from *The Tempest* (I.ii.16, 224).

CONTENTS

—scapes welcome young birds—

—Louis Zukofsky, "A"-22

WHITHER

—heelprint and halter, halfway
heard: before means back

then, to know before
it breaks it lurches

so in the snowfield's
stalk- and stem-broken

edges a rosehip bends,
reddens at its tip:

halfway across, near dusk,
to know snow before

this is nothing to
naming this unread surface

defect of drift lines:
snow breaks the back

of the field it
possesses, which is nine

points of the law:
ultimate elements ultimately break

wended laws, and if
scrolls of wind darling

us inversely to their
pressures, or demand discovery

before thaw, what holocene
disasters captivate a snowfield:

to hazard the arctic
or cast me aside

but snow's lien on
those curios I covet

confounds the verge of
implication: entire stuttering routs

break halfway to before
or snow snooze-buttons

the day before day
can chase itself down

LANDSCAPE

An inspected geography leans in with the landscape's repetitions.

—Bob Perelman, *a.k.a.*

I see you with the
landscape that I am.

—Alice Notley, *At Night the States*

Trepanned: in other words, my mind wanders
no farther than the map I drew from memory,

marking the stone-circled embers memory makes smoke
—wisps to occlude whatever arrow-line I'd draw next.

Next is the legend: asterisk for tree, speck for settlement,
double dagger for ruins, circled star for fallen star,

wave of my hand for broken satellite, exhalation for
exhalation spent climbing the rise step by step

toward the form of the field, the retirement of assent.
Here lake, here site of ambush, here fallen king.

The thistle's tendency—its bent posture—toward the oracular.
The wolf's basking ruse.

I'm not fixin' to get rowdy, venture
off-radar, fuck with open source code: spring

hills of squills, the rarefied checkout line,
the tiny guest bedroom still undusted

since winter: we've formed our truces today.
The technological wonders beetle

away from words: real refinement
urges a pass, and what, I ask,

does anyone want? Discovery creeps
wormwardly along a mathematics

of mingling my mother warned me about—
anyway, in the beautiful valley

my haloed seeing rues transparency,
shoos such likelihood aft, away: I yawn,

yearn, perceiving only how vertigo
secretaries me into the office.

If musket-ball honeycombs fog
        and enlacens lines, if rivers rule

out the rules
        of topography

and cul-de-sac traceries share
        shadows with hypnosis through
discards and nothings:

                or if someplace other
teaches thinness of presence,

        a track that wanders coastally
through radio schematics and wingtip

among dark, over darker
        latitudes and interruptions,

        the footage of tendencies
and corporeal inarticulations, a

time for sound alone
            to quiver assembled lives

A suicide raid from thinnest branches:
phantom census of provincial ghosts

—so the edge of being
disintegrates blind hunches

and the only thing between us
is subdivided sky.

Whatever mumbled get-go gets
counted against what's otherwise

only space enough for a figure:
an interval chiseled from decades,

some salvaged discrepancy, wandered
here among other dusts.

An echo's answer: repeat after me. This is only
an interrogation of the bullet

The bullet fragmented in memory of a hit song and we

We collected at the bedside of our friend. Her name
was kindness, a kind of violence,
or caused kind violence—

I'd prefer a recording of silence

A fear of the future

In the holy city we live inside the wall,
in the shadow of the wall

Stone-bent, bed-kept, smack in the middling smoke

We sleep homesickly and leave verse at the door
in the wall, the frayed end. I am less interested in

a peek at the garments of understanding,
to fingerprint their cloth,
than to have once worn them.

Whatever leftovers of night I might
     claim: grit, lunar halo, edge of profile
or another fence to let in the cold:
     two days later, a survivor replaces   .
everything: the door that opens or starts
     with a single word emboldens scriptures
of snow slipped into the house to blank
     the house, a laziness of trees outside
that distracts, an ancient pluck to forget
     intention's fool voice, affection's cruel move
to some atonal stomping grounds: because
     I left I legended not return but
the parallel desire, emptied and
     unbothered: so winter's vivid window
you watch through exceeds the telling surface
     or the holdings, the brief entries honored
with skipping sounds: your scrutiny alters
     the field unfilled with wanting, slippages
stun-gunned to snowpiles, or my shaky heart's
     cancellations level the hassles I've
inherited: to dismantle a breath
     until a bargain subdues it, come home

The landscape remains obedient to previous notions. It is Massachusetts outside my window and Massachusetts in my mind: it is only the site of some larger omission. The landscape an open system of fires, a naive word's wound, a trick made of phone wires and a waiting breath. The asphalt taught me as asphalt always teaches, friction and burn, all rough texture. I thought it misfortune, not remedy—a crumpled cardinal's red feathers in the road. I crammed for hours to learn to predict this weather, to memorize the shape of the overslept-on pillow, to balance my bicycle and my checking account, to locate the surge in my chest, to plot a course even this far. Make it in Massachusetts.

I built a frame around the landscape, to shape it in a way more sympathetic to its own inclinations. Built up hills to crown what one gazing on them might stutter. Built hollows below the hills to catch the wind's harvest.

Once I could see clouds, the instructions seemed clearer than the sky. When I breathed, clouds would shift. When I held breath clouds would shift.

Built a frame around the landscape, to shape my own inclinations. Cut grasses that never would have hidden much. Held a forked stick and wished for water. At the edge of the frame, I leaned over to see what was beyond. A boy walked through the landscape, counting quietly the numbers of stars that had sparked while I shut my eyes.

Dumb winter cannot be proved
by heavy branches
or light-fraught roof-holes
to say myself sleepily
the clanging resemblances
turning upon this field
but for the obligations of barest
chance and the pocket soliloquies
or how the wind rushed
its unaccomplished digressions

So: halogen noontime: a covert life
lives a reluctance and scraps farewell: that

old inside, obligingly, whatever
flush of sun otherwise unmoved:

the day won't reconcile its recessive light:
a perimeter's bleed: interface of hill-

side and skyline obliges: dyad
of bodies: where there's one there's another:

overtaken day: and day parachutes
and settles: bewildered sun-sick bulb

The weather was sent off with a thank-you-
for-your-donations-of-pity. I had

larger purposes: hoardings of myself
and other withheld raptures, the sidearm

program condensed to a kind of horseplay.
I stuck to my story. Now my late-day

body unravels into a looted
lesson: affinities jackknifed apart

reveal the ardors of homesickness.
But purity of intent in any

form is a parting of praise from a wee-
hours' insouciance. A divestment.

It's easier to believe this than to
disperse the world I see into cluttered

freight. The marriage of urge and precedent,
overlapping among spike-split trees, renews

itself with scant attention, bruises me
with its fidelity to specifics:

I've always lacked such tendencies: so if
new weather replaces these needs with loans

of billowed geometry, ribcage-raw,
remanent: or if life daggers us most

thoroughly in its suspended moments,
grant me a witness: let my injuries

bed down amid the bungled like slo-mo
pleasures shaken from troubled instruments—

broken electrons, mineral beauties!
At least the strictly factual remains,

another barrel I'm bent over, an
alias of evitability.

How anymore hooky
in highrise field, failed
without force of failure:

I sured you—
gallopway down-
town
I'd go
muddy-roaded,
in dithers, a truck
window-perplexed—

f'r instance:

I'd cantle song and skill
to the barn-wood
whens,

slushy gray, tire-tracked:
bring back
this busted even-
ing, the hilly town
ditched

I traffic in the elided spaces
inside my head, the ineluctable
tangent, the staid dust-bunnies of belief:

I count on the one thing I can't count on,
and oh I admire the anecdotal
country, the packed luggage of inertia

offering the bed's critique of resolve
and difficulties. I'm only looking
for some average fun. Once I took care

of taking care, I had little left
to worry about, but a sense of relief
emerged mostly from being overlooked.

Such chronic scraps wangle, shimmy:
an endless F.A.Q. I skimmed, at best.

The runaway habitations: last week's river-bends, the squeaky hub of landscape. A horizon persists. If there are limits to what our insomniac preparations allow, the past rebuilds the sky and I endure the absence of another dilemma. The lesser smudge of morning doesn't mean I can believe a vision over valleys, or a man slowly bending down to pat some appealing story. But a foreign wreckage escapes the same simplicities, faded emblems of historical accident: the roadside border house lofts unoccupied plots.

Unable to recall the proper technology, I imagine the
counterfeit gesture. Winter targets the branches. A frozen
sequence swells. Birds peep. Grass needles—tiny music.
Wind tries to return to the sky some pigment.

No, birds stir and disperse in the molecular wind. And
why shouldn't they? A skeletal bush's snagged tinsel alters
the light. The country is ancient: absence of radio voices,
rusted altars, flowers' exploded and spent blooms. Even
snow brittle. The thicket's assembly.

A would for wooing: let desire derange the browses and reckless residencies of memory, the dialogue of origin and ear, this chronicle of unmouthed and twilit imminences. I sought some other kneeling inexactitude to fathom, some scumbled mash-up of whoops and whimpers, wedded wounds, backtrack badges suffused with defect and frisson. A homeless cadence. But the fairy-tale self plea-bargains a lesser sentence.

I wanted to molest a field, fondle its fronds, tickle fallen leaves, finger its weeds and hummocks, pull up some roots, scrape away a little dirt, see what was hidden. Maybe I would take it behind the woods and hoist it into my lap, blow ripples through the tips of its grass, taste all that chlorophyll. Green grow the rushes? I needed to know, but need was not word enough to contain the gush of this growth. I brought a six-pack of pale ale to set a mood, but the winds blew out while I dawdled and drank. A moon came and went. My shyness gained coherence.

I hazarded a ravening twang:

the rough drafts of laundry-lines
a ballad for the daylight,

the dusty coherences
of getting better:

it might be about
leaf-pressed distant
other room recall,

the wist influences,
cinders, a fugitive
willingness:

our shared sense
of idiom,

our reeded risk

Scratch within branches of branches within
wind: trauma longs along these upstart lines.
Legacies of late sunlight organize
the atomic: lesser complaints folded
into the social, what-gives aftermath
of habit—substitute fugue, grass-shadowed sweek.

Waiting not in the sense of wanting to
leave, to the forthward drowsy element,
some surly specific: but in the path,
from this pause, to bellbroken almanac
and windblown memory, frequented facts
or some other sensible loneliness.

At home in the lean-to, my renewal succumbed
to pared bones, paired pistols

strafing the beached remains,
the beach's sifted sources:

bits of shell flaked and tinny, a raw skin.

The footpath I followed
here is irreversible,

let us say,
speaking slowly,

calling the blue that awaits puberty

or puberty was a pony I rode till sunset
then pitched my tent in a parking lot.

And so I retired to the potato-chip factory,
or retired from it—

Though I am hardly industrious,
here is my industrial refuse:
enough smoke as might fill
a thousand cardboard boxes.

It was always easy to find lunch,

and I practiced thanksgiving, gift giving,
the gist of an outlook,
foiled crimp that refuses opening.

My appetite? Forget such encyclopedia,
such come-and-gone, the hourly
wage that eagers itself
across the manager's desk.

After the brief night:
to overidentify
with sublimated edges,

testimony of familiar
voices and unbewildered
light.

Across the river,
none of these suggest
the little place looking

it up or taking answer.
The tree cracked
and collapsed

to the inventory
of cigarettes and fenceposts.

The minimal mapping:

some vast affection

of unexpected presences: it is
possible recencies

that order the hand,

the grass colorless,
seeded and scorched:

a dust of falling things
and a dust of rising things,

a rivered eyesight

blowing pines:
but past us

move
slackened echoes

Nothing betrays nothing, nor
truss of lipread nothing-
in-particulars, rustic
and numinous:
velocity's skin-split souvenir,
pistilled hymns
in gunglinting profile
to disarm oneself further
from hallowed mistake.

Ruined increment, knot,
needle not kept:
a day intends
less than lit, up-pointed
airs, the habitual limits
of summoning: need nestles
close—limbed-out or
remnant thwartings, days-done
if nothing furnaces nothing.

Explain it to me, central Pennsylvania: how the elderly woman's daybreak humming articulates the spill of dogwood petals over the backyard's blocked F-250, the wind's tenor in our heads. (I've forgotten my lines again.) Yes, the warblers have returned to the tree-screened creeks, the flea market vendors set out their ragged exhibits for our fingers, and we too can gun-barrel a lecture to the sky, or wave at the tractor-trailers rushing along these trails.

The house was built in the image of a house: stick by stick, stones unearthed—something recognizable. Sure, the walls buckled. This window's a lapse in the bedroom, though through it you can see the Masonic Temple, the Biffburger's orange façade, a kennel of barking beagles. (Forgive the damp basement—aren't they all?—and the coal chute's lack of coal.) Even on a rainy day we found what we needed in low-shot cloud and asphalt scribble, but lost the gist of our arguments in the fluency of lawns along this sidestreet. I wanted less a sense of space than to exert a reason for my arm's reach. I mean, the second time we encountered summer we refused it, and the memory of a previous July mattered less than the refusal. One could say poverty was what we wanted all along.

What will waterproof the resentments? In a silent northern way, infinity monochromes the question of comfort. I pin hesitations under the weather: raw tuft, gray ice, a scattered rest amid an indoor rain. My previously knuckled rationalities catch your mended half-lives, the process of drift drawn close. Is it gesture we mean, an offhand overlap, some signature in skies? Darkness brushes up on history: the flickering lamp flickers on. But for the bootleg of this confused and humble evening, the truer testament erodes a getaway. The land lies itself to sleep.

A tangled blank exults:
such singular tatters.

The weather holds
the capacity of retreat:
and ditches brimming
with ourselves, a just-
resting vocabulary
of hideout
and exile: words
enter eaves,
some trickledown
lyrics window-thin:
shadow beneath juniper
or parked car,
inland legerdemain
to trouble meltwater
and perforate the lines
behind the dopplered drift
and the fact of
culling: daylight spoke:
or, unsaid, it grows tall,
aging earlier than turning
to semi-real animals
or fissured dreams

That woolgathered import
manages some leeway,
a facsimile
of fetching: I'm
using my head
to head off a telling,
the mobile
home in dull hours
undesigned:
the inner life
has fled responsibilities
of forgetting,
occasions for impression:
so antic irrevocability
bypasses what we might
stand, x'es out the obvious
to waltz weightless
among stripped ponderosa:
yes, the bluntness
of the landscape,
after awhile:

Crown of character, I dis-hire you. I will muddle within the copse.

I solved you only as a simple scratch of a him against a her. Something perhaps broken. Mere splinter of listening. Cast out. Native. A burden. A winter.

I banged my me against your us. A germ of being. Slack scraps.

My bearing: bent. My blather: blurred. My blot of understanding. My abrasions. My pocket economy.

My own dereliction.

The rural equation of slanted refrain
glazes discomposed weeds:

a backyard relic, a whittled insufficiency
named by forlorn anatomies.

The clever answer: metallic
highway harmonics otherwise

nonstop in lower, colder instants:
so the lashworn tumble veers.

A time-elapsed plea: our inventive ethics allow us to put some English on a nomenclature of need. Massage it a little, hassle these jagged humidities. The country no longer exists, and I'll pop the clutch and peel out as declaration I now know I'm on the losing team. Call mine a drive-by melancholy. The evening's hollow earth theories bore me. The lace of being has outgrown itself and exalts these field recordings with a lifetime warranty.

Someplace in its enterprise, the recent
rests, still unfound, awaiting its end
in a signal ineloquently lost
amid these periodic bankruptcies.
Of the through-and-through's time
being, the lessened said nothing.

The leftover commitments of old
amnesias tailor low-mountained
suitabilities: no, I didn't stay
anything, nor measure the momentum.

To eke afar from trouble,
I don't thumb
a generous selfhood

*

The luxuries, unmapped,
the states' bloom:
a two-day reason held

If everything belongs to something
else, we become who we want to be
imagined by, and sunlight
slants sideways over the earth
like simultaneous excruciations.
This landscape can no longer
hold itself together.

A rustle explains the underbrush in a gum-snapped metrics: I beat around the parking lot for two hours to find an uncrowded corner. The runoff bled there. Kept going. The sky rejected a siege of fancies and aircraft. Clouds merely cooled, congealed. They are not meant as pleasant relief. Further forays yielded no more than expected—mere muttering doubt, a delicately feral borderlands. Forget watching and waiting, prophecy's kicks, the cavernous echo of streetlit exteriors. And fuck this conversation with the natural: I can't outlast the outdoors. I'm raising a pennant for a brittle self.

On clouds' crumpled page, a winter water-
mark of sun. Houses lean on wind, another

transient body within an unbound
spill of smoke, soot to smudge hills. A clutter

gates the raw fence of woods where trees rake
air, what wind can carry—dust, leaves, paper

scraps which tell no story but that of tangled flight.
The hills ring, delimit a sense of risk. Seen, here,

from above, asphalt's conduit sends and receives,
retrieves passing messages, overheard whispers

we cannot quite decipher. Along its edges
are scattered cast-off rags, torn strips of rubber.

In the blowth, half-jingled, honeycomb
of nascent scrip: witted whereall
night falls bumbling aloud,
a coppice's uptipped accent
middles, roofliply, in the smattered nulls.
A bitten bark worsts the tongue
of erratic air: overlapping, are we
not foxed to tremble, royaling so?
The list of loosened luck buckles here,
appling the slopes to rue a rill: hemlock
hatches of steeples awry, the energy
refiners: such frail scatter, vagrant elations.

The history of the country—less
emblematic noise than lustrous cravings—
allows an outline: continuity
of dwelling in its inward signs incants
the dust, and a two-headed arrow points
where we are ours. Props to the posse we
rode in with, shout-outs to deformations,
let us whim them as they beckon backward.

Immortalities overlap these squalls
of stranded selves: are we not cottaging
before the altar of the bearable
or gung-ho on the boardwalk?
Shunt the stuck-to days writing the lives
of the land: I omen you. You deften me.

There is no ideal blackout
or validation of passage

A conversion narrative:
rain's complicated phrases

Mingle of us frailly
mattering

Precarious annal and
some finished proof

INSCAPE

Held a flat thornback. Even, a rather,
the untended gizmo: imply less
tree than tried, surfeit of surmised
selves: torn. Withers atop a weather
within, a name says a saw was.
There is thin and thin to think of it,
divisions part hidden, subduals
of sway: slash of branch, swing of twig,
sworn-off spoke, straw of year, scuff, part:
broke in the brake. So hover, hull, hear:
such bang-up schisms, radar letters
to what leaves. Green bolts in hills' heat: nub
and quick, windy and wracked, pulls a slip:
a furl limns tips split, a sleaving, slift.

Ten leaves amidden mast the hammering
yaws. Ware wind their color: florid stipple,
trebly grain. Frisky linens, these, bough-banked
or sun-maimed, unroomed, yare: don't call me
woodsome, wish of dust-deer risen, ghostly
continuance: so bereft, bypass spells,
curl. Willing undoes wanting, mazer than me.
Fettle the unlasted, embered other
in rash of burnt furze: flapper, a forethought,
bloom of timing to feaze percussive
memory. Airy swap, camlet cloak, go:
it isn't want of finish that fetches
fiery loft, shivering glaze in full dusk:
may fables of enclosure wish otherwise.

ESCAPE

Torque of tongue,
twiddled: starched
shortcomings
and -goings:
when you run
the wind follows
you, falls blistered
and burnt: hand-
writing allows
such green timber
to ruin knife-knit
openings: the tip
directs touch, torch
of swollen remainders:
but reason rides rescue,
keeps askance
the flashlit forest,
faded swale,
bracken, crook
rivered unwillingly
to banked myths:
some stillness
skirts the swell

What, stuttering, fails toward touch:

the leafshot friability
or undeclared quiet of sticks
shortwaved

a season's sum of latches
and zero itinerance:
sufficient priors hem a lure—

beyond a briarneck, lapse
turns light: turl and sumac-twist:
how this stretch bees

rooted redundancies
race to pattern it

These scabbed leaves loosely north,
landslipped: otherwhorled in vacancies
of bough-bladed stripling—

Lonesome intention, riven match:
boon of brazen dismantlings takes
amid later light: underwinged.

SUMMER LETTERS

the way memory and summer
reveal their terrible affinities
while speaking separate dialects

—Michael Davidson, "Summer Letters"

1.

shored up inside still
they speak liturgies over
this valley's grid

and does summer remain
in a sort of air
or a morning

it is a fact
limited views on days like these
pursuing burnt earth

and when he returned
a lampglow
fluttered papers

the house leaned and he
did not imagine summer
hills fading into white lines

2.

returning we burned ourselves
and in our books burned

star fine ash sketches
paper imprints

his breath the collage of speech
his breaks culled never
his hands left marks all over this town

perception returns
on returning forgets
endures fathoms years
fashions speech's garb

skin masks pale stars

3.

its name begins at the lake
regrets the insides of clouds
and gulls so far inland

windows open only partway
color has already been written
and what won't resolve

reminders in asphalt
loom
shouldered into simply describing
twenty years ago
twenty minutes from now
which is entangled

early morning
word spreads

4.

unhitched
dust settles

water assumes the shapes of rocks
the haze and a hand on a page
a heron stands in the creek

by night they wait for another
mapping a route from home
scant furtive fires

nothing but in care of you
his arms in this sad knot
scans hems trees

hinge upon a past upon
an unseen gift a cloud
suspended behind a chimney

and to speak a lantern apart
they followed traces
in the attraction of habit

5.

everything has slowed
climbed steps to the door
and hid behind it
is it possible to turn
another disappears all
of the sky is a ruse is a
letter is a day grown over

seeks emphasis in calendars
many hours spoke

vows ignite the memory
prove intention how it
presumes

the recurring sun and patch
of hills the voice from corners
thorns successive designs
weather became important
creased lines bleed
dispatches
to think of drift

blackly treed vein
crevices

dialogues drown
a nest
unutterable

6.

to hedge's green layers
we turned a twig
roots of my woolgathering

speaks to the beginning
or two years back
the pulse in winds
dwells atop silent house
Oneonta countrymen
roots of the beginning
of dusty lines awakened
the leaves' silver ends

remembered through memory
how often the grass bent
and boards cracked

and when he returned
returning forgot

paled into another

7.

shapes impressed upon pillows by mourning
lost words a waking promise spreads and now all
ceremonies have ended curled his wings grew from
a knee from cock wilson the historic ward numbers
cadences concealed absence he begged a copse hid
such messages an idea of age gathers any missing
story so well hewed we hunted water and leaves and
stones three creeks silty walked another riverbank
once our vocabularies now halved

8.

a warning of moon in daylight on summer's quiet
paths yet waning to cold air she revealed hitherto
abandoned structures clove pendant spoken with
burnt tongue under fog calls each departed letter and
the letters spelled a name in these hills and words
passed between two houses a mile apart a mark
crosses and begins in each letter another writes

9.

water parts two roads to words' white circle

candles burned under hills the length of this country
driven from the letter of the intent to what's left of
a pattern pressed between leaves

lost light to away maybe we forgot he said push
mist the road blink left rose a summer ending in
rain Dutch river settlements

terrel unfold ways begin dark a seacoast faints on
falling this press acre of ground we moved through
return paths feet cut down

10.

into sight abandons senses and voices sway. the hill
once painted fades and eyelashes occur as dusk. fields
grown over unseen a hollow fills. the lake dirt

in afterthought begins a sentence
     envelopes drifted tables

and letters accumulate unsent. two voices
     events, events
     the mornings begin

damp grass fenced skin peeling
I unburying all year

SUMMER'S TENANTS

Solitude is not an absolute number, though if I outlast another night counting on my fingers, it may begin to seem that way. The hedge outside grows nearly as fast as I can prune it, though I prefer to rely on the pity of passersby rather than the fickleness of my own sunlit instincts. And my ladder won't reach the tallest branches. Objects disappear within the foliage for days at a time, then reappear on the lawn when I least expect. Superstitious, I'm just as happy to hide behind my hedge, gathering whatever folklore I can find, as to peer through that alliance of branches and leaves at the road.